MILLENNIAL PROGNOSTICATIONS

other books by the author

POETRY
Dawn Visions
Burnt Heart/Ode to the War Dead
This Body of Black Light Gone Through the Diamond
The Desert is the Only Way Out
The Chronicles of Akhira
Halley's Comet
Awake as Never Before
The Ramadan Sonnets
The Blind Beekeeper
Mars & Beyond
Laughing Buddha Weeping Sufi
Salt Prayers
Ramadan Sonnets (The Ecstatic Exchange revised edition)
Psalms for the Brokenhearted
I Imagine a Lion
Coattails of the Saint
Abdallah Jones and the Disappearing-Dust Caper
Love is a Letter Burning in a High Wind
The Flame of Transformation Turns to Light
Underwater Galaxies
The Music Space
Cooked Oranges
Through Rose Colored Glasses
Like When You Wave at a Train and the Train Hoots Back at You
In the Realm of Neither
The Fire Eater's Lunchbreak
Millennial Prognostications

THEATER / THE FLOATING LOTUS MAGIC OPERA COMPANY
The Walls Are Running Blood
Bliss Apocalypse

PROSE
Zen Rock Gardening
The Little Book of Zen
Zen Wisdom

MILLENNIAL PROGNOSTICATIONS

POEMS

November 25, 1999 - February 2, 2000

Daniel Abdal-Hayy Moore

The Ecstatic Exchange
2009
Philadelphia

Millennial Prognostications
Copyright © 2009 Daniel Abdal-Hayy Moore
All rights reserved.
Printed in the United States of America

For quotes any longer than those for critical articles and reviews, contact:
The Ecstatic Exchange,
6470 Morris Park Road, Philadelphia, PA 19151-2403
email: abdalhayy@danielmoorepoetry.com

First Edition
ISBN: 978-0-578-00773-1 (paper)
Published by *The Ecstatic Exchange*,
6470 Morris Park Road, Philadelphia, PA 19151-2403

Also available from *The Ecstatic Exchange*:
Knocking from Inside, poems by Tiel Aisha Ansari

I would like to aknowledge with deepest gratitude the help of Abdallateef (Ian) Whiteman who designed the first 18 books of the Ecstatic Exchange Series, and Larry Didona who helped me make the transition to design by author.

Cover collage by the author
Back cover photograph by Peter Sanders

DEDICATION

To
the memory of Mexican Poet
Marco Antonio Montes de Oca (1932-2009),

the radiance of Shaykh Muhammad ibn al-Habib of Fez
(and the continuation of the Habibiyya),
Shaykh Bawa Muhaiyuddeen,
all shuyukh of instruction and ma'arifa
and
Baji Tayyaba Khanum
of the unsounded depths

✳

*The earth is not bereft
of Light*

CONTENTS

Author's Introduction   8

PART 1
As We Enter the 3rd Millennium   13
All Utterances Shall Be Prophetic   15
Prognostication Rare and Sweet   17
In Simplicity and Complexity   19
The Dawn Comes Up a Very Planetarium Blue   21
Sober Interlude   22
First Came the End of the World   25
The Night Showers Multicolored Sparks   27
Time the Trickster Machine   28
I Praise You and I Prize You   31
The Mystery of Someone Sleeping   33
There Are a Thousand Pastures   36
I Lean Out Over the Balcony of My Bed   38
Squirrel-Scratch   40
Predictions   42
Around the Feet of the Lord   45
Meticulous in Their Apprehension Moving   47

PART 2
Multiple Languages Multiple Ritual Gestures   51
Kaleidoscope   52
Late and Lovely   57
On the High Seas   59
Down at the Corner Grocer   62
Down the Long Road   63

Way Down in Mississippi   65
I Got Shot to Death   68
Love Song   70

We're a Tribe of Fish Head Navigators   73
Lips Can't   74
The Cloth That Refused to be Washed   76
First Millennial Blizzard   80
And of All the Ten Thousand Things   82

AUTHOR'S INTRODUCTION

As I write this in January of 2009, we mark nearly a decade after the fabulous and celebrated turn of the century, wondering if a new era has begun that improves upon the 20th century, or a worrisomely worse one that already has revealed enormous challenges of wars on many fronts, African famine and genocide, Middle Eastern tragedy (and genocide) and in the United States, a serious financial collapse that threatens at this early date to only get worse. And it was only a very short time after the millennial change that one of the most world-shifting events happened that among other things has affected world travel and inspired other rogue terrorists who pathologically believe they are doing God's bidding: 9/11/2001.

But this is also an historic moment (as I write this in my Philadelphia studio downstairs and a nighttime rainstorm can be heard dripping outside my window) on the eve of the Inauguration of Barack Hussein Obama as our 44th President. This event in itself could be the beginning of a new era, certainly for the United States, and hopefully and possibly for the world, after eight years of hell with the (rogue) regime of George W. Bush & Cheney, and their Neo Conservative cohorts and thugs who longed to remake the world in their own image and have largely brought the very Devil's face upon it by their outrageous unleashings. But President Obama, the first president of color in our country's history, and truly a mind-boggling and renaissance event that has the potential to turn not only this country inside-out for the healing of its own scandalous history, but also to change not only the image but also the policy of this country throughout the world. Is this a "prognostication?" No, but it is a passionate hope, and perhaps a vision of the first arc of a wave from the turn of the century to further along in the century, which will be up against unprecedentedly global odds, and of course a bumpy ride here at home as well (not in my house, God willing, which in the lovely old Chinese Poet tradition, is an abode of peace and contemplation).

So I wrote this book of poems up to and through the actual New Year from 1999 to 2000, and having videotaped the celebrations worldwide, wrote as if in shorthand the worldwide national events as they were happening in flash images as they passed by (see *Kaleidoscope*), with a tip of the hat to Allen Ginsberg with his bop prosody and snapshot poetics.

But this is not a book of poetic futuristics, oracle-like I-Ching yarrow-stick or coin countings or consciousness Tarot readings, nothing so formal nor formulated. Perhaps its "prognostication" aspect is in trying to be open-hearted and sense-aware of images and their meanings, or meanings and their images, as they occur in the world both most immediate to us and by extension universal and even cosmic, detail by detail, focusing on what Blake called "minute particulars." It's a kind of lengthy prayer with sidebars, digressions and returns, hopefully each time more earnestly to the Source of all and of Whom, as it was said by the Prophet Muhammad, peace of Allah be upon him, *"Do not curse time, for time is Allah…"*

Enough said.

January 7, 2009

They do not know how immortal, but I know.
— *Walt Whitman*

PART 1

AS WE ENTER THE 3rd MILLENNIUM

As we enter the 3rd millennium
roots reach down like gnarled hands
boats rise up on waves like ballerinas
buildings bloom like flower gardens
skies turn purple then gray
then yellow-gold then white as a sheet
for a split second on everyone's eyelids
and astounding things take place in them

Saith Tiresias
sitting full weight on a miniature city of sugar in
robes of flame or flame retardant
cerulean satin
his long dark face an enigma in a space where
everything else is openly plain and simple

Birds fly through slack telephone wires making their
casual auguries first
one direction then veering off at an angle into another

Ants carry and are carrying on as usual
unmindful of the year's *embrasure*
which may be a new word I'm coining because I
can't think of one momentous or
all-encompassing enough radical in its
edgelessness right at the
razor's edge of things metamorphosing into
entities rare and strange at the
sound of the millennial bell or at least the

wooden sound of the clapper inside the
bell since the reverberations of the glassy brass
bell itself will resound all the
way through the 3rd millennium
to the fourth

when wingéd horses may be as commonplace as cars or
thought transportation eyesight itself
able to teleport us to far-off places and
straunge strondes as Chaucer that
early second millennium
observer of human foibles would say and his
strange words tumbling through the lengthy and
wildly troubled centuries to us still

11/25

ALL UTTERANCES SHALL BE PROPHETIC

All utterances shall be prophetic
on the tongues of brown round-faced children with silver eyes

and snow shall fall in glass balls
onto miniature cities of sugar

and the seas shall rise a fraction
and the skies shall darken

and the skies shall lighten as before
nothing remains the same
but the days go on as usual
around the next corner
and the sharp one after that
where a procession of feather-bedecked magistrates and
city elders of the
emerging metropolises of the imagination will suddenly
heave into view playing on
exotic instruments made of bamboo and wound grass blades
and singing the most
outlandish things such as

"The house of air shall be everywhere"

"The light at night shall be more bright"

"Every third person shall be a saint"

"I miss seeing your face

beaming down onto mine"

and other phrases both
poignant and unexpected

as everything else is

                                                                      11/25

PROGNOSTICATION RARE AND SWEET

Prognostication rare and sweet
when what we do is see what's here

the locomotive through the bedroom wall
the cellar full of green ghosts and the
   attic full of brown bric-a-brac
fruit that fills the window with its
   gleaming skin
goats chewing sideways on the rug
puffs of smoke that spell out all these
     poor devices

the very air we breathe sweet honey
spun from heavenly hives

Next day of the new millennium is the
same as the day before you get up if you're

still alive as always look out or in through
shining eyes see what's there and
what to do drink your water eat your
daily bread and thank the

Giver of all sly delectable things

You're not here long in any scenario
the scenario and all your flesh is
   whisked away and you

go on down Gossamer Road into a place so far of
imprecise description but except for the
flamey one is said to be better than
this one with its

tornadoes earthquakes divorce-rate and
all the rest including millennial fever
insecurities that rise to the top like scum at the
turn of a thousand years every day a

possible crack in the way of things through which
we might need a parachute to effect
soft landing

God unperturbed at One and at
home in all these flutterings a blue
everywhere endlessly emanating from around Him

singing His praises

11/27

IN SIMPLICITY AND COMPLEXITY

In simplicity and complexity pure rotation
    simply and complexly flows
the barren desert can't be barren with so many sand grains
      tossed and turned

The sky goes on and on until it hits a
    planetary sphere a solid moon a
pure rotation just like the one at home
turning round the central table where
brocade sleeves on crook'd elbows are
    lined up like curtains on
        gilded windows

Tables where the laws are searched out and explained
by the learnéd doctors of the stars
the seed puts out its fragile feather and extends it
the larva turns and turns inside its case
    awaiting meteorological auspiciousness
to emerge triumphant as a fruit fly
or butterfly now creasing the air of the
    rain forest into morpho winkings of

opening and closing wings as it
works its way to whatever it works its way to
to be satisfied as a
morpho butterfly with its
    shocking midnight blue against the

surrounding transparencies of air

rotation and rotation and rotation

      everywhere

                                                11/27

THE DAWN COMES UP A VERY PLANETARIUM BLUE

The dawn comes up a very planetarium blue
red tinged at the lower edge

Little birds are untucking their heads and shaking their
sleepy brains awake
cockroaches are running for cover

Somewhere a murderer is nervously washing his
knife looking over his shoulder

Somewhere lovers are turning in each other's arms
hating the day

Somewhere a Bodhissatva is looking at
nothingness from Nothingness' standpoint
through slitted eyes and smiling

A ship is sinking coffee cups rolling on the floor
a deer is licking her doe awake long black tongue
my own eyes are burning from being awake too
    long
my heart is brimming with the circling
      lariat of this song
trying to not try to let the song lines
        come through on their own

as the sky now is a more
uniform whitish wash of blue

11/28

SOBER INTERLUDE

for Raheem Bath

As I took my morning walk today
in the woods at the end of our city street
over brown and yellow autumn leaves
soaked to the dirt from last night's pounding rain
dark spindly limbs bare where before they
bore such leaves as those I was walking on

and thought of the young man dead today of the
same furious pneumonia that cut Jim Hensen down
in a surprise Sherman's March of bacillus through the
delicate netting of his lungs only
twenty years old

and even though I didn't know him not even
sure which of the young men in our community he was
(though I know which one his mother is lamenting now)
and as my feet trod the packed leaves and hard-packed
earth of the trail on which so
many feet have trod and will trod after I'm gone
the rocks and stones in their Wordsworthian diurnal course
the whole planet whirling round

my walk to the crest of the same hill I try to
walk every day my consciousness carried there on these
shod feet and thought of the little
commissioned book on the Buddha I'm writing
his revelation that

everything that arises ceases everything that has an
origin ends everything that
lives dies those we
know and those we don't know the
exceedingly handsome and bright as well as the
dull and misshapen
each prince as well as each gnat that
breathes the air or passes through it on its
way somewhere this

boy in North Carolina away from his family at college
living his life face front full of
high spirits and hope

dead at 10 p.m. last night in a hospital bed
no longer able to breathe

and how death is at the center of all our poems
touchstone of our inspiration just as
God is at the center of our lives from
Whom we come and to Whom we all return

That when those much older than us die we lose part of our past
That when those much younger than us die we lose part of our future

That when I die and go back to Him

this hill will continue the same as before winter trees bare
summer trees full of leaves hard earth hard rocks
a consciousness gazing there across to the
opposite side aware of the

weather and the slippery uphill wintry climb
or the summery climb through
sticky briars and vines
same witness to what forever is
God's strong Holy Light when
all the leaves have fallen

and all the feet that
trod on them have gone

11/28

FIRST CAME THE END OF THE WORLD

First came the end of the world then the
    beginning
for the end was in the beginning

like taking a sweater off backwards over your head

everything pulled through itself backwards so fast things move

well not exactly forwards horses'
hooves clattering backwards over paving stones couples
framed in windows in backwards embraces
ubiquitous yellow a buttery

yellow hue to the air the whole sky even
roasted-butter-colored the whole

universe suddenly collapsed into its
first nanosecond as well as its penultimate
ping in a ring around our
second finger from the right on the right hand
like the rings of Saturn that most

interesting and somehow friendly and
familiar of planets always at a rakish tilt
with its buttery rings how we manage to

carry on in a world that is
constantly being pulled through itself thus is a

wonder how people can
procreate plan
careers throw big parties on yachts or in
basements while great chugging

chunks of mysterious reversaling spaces are passing us by like
landscapes out a freeway window

and our hearts as fragile as flocks of pigeons taking
off together in a kind of
möbius strip that brings them
back to the roof again having
circled the trees and back alleys and
flapped gray wings in a gray wintry sky that is
no longer buttery circling

like the circularity of the end and
beginning in the same ring

Milky froth on my moustache as its
hairs poke black and white wires through in

utter growth's forward motion

12/14

THE NIGHT SHOWERS MULTICOLORED SPARKS

The night showers multicolored sparks over the
ark's bow as it
plows through the stars

Velvet night night of beneficence night
without equal singular as a pin held straight
up in the dark with its sharp tip

Many faces crowd forward to look
the crowd opens a space
the object of their burning eyes and curious faces

Earth like a blue jeweled ball suspended in black velvet

Velvet night night of beneficence night
without equal night showering

multicolored sparks over the

ark's bow as it

plows through the stars

12/17

TIME THE TRICKSTER MACHINE

I've got a trickster clock one of those
old-fashioned black plastic Felix the Cat clocks with
rolling eyes missing its tail
sometimes it keeps perfect time sometimes it's
half a day off or more

I unplugged it for a while after I
found out plus it made a little
grinding noise I thought was
rain coming down the drain
but plugged it back in thinking I don't
care if it's completely wrong I love it
rolling eyes missing tail squeak squeak

Now the forum is swept clean and the
senators have all left and
Caesar's a lump of cloth death folded like the
folds of his brain in the great
toga he wore now drenched in
blood that wraps him like a thrown-out forgotten thing

Time is a hair as long as it grows

A gaze as long as God's love guides its eyes

Time is a heartbeat as great as the ocean's horizon

Time is a black letter written in black ink and
sent through the dark to its blind receiver

I mention Caesar and his carnal loneliness
as a time-splice that fits into this
moment's dimension along with other
historical moments that may or may
not have taken place at least as we
think of them

George Washington had a swan's head
Jean d'Arc rode an invisible horse into battle
The first men and women looked at the
dawn breaking and sang polyphonic song

Perhaps it's the missing tail that throws the clock off
a pendulous swing calculated in its precision
timing mechanism to help it keep perfect time

This room is revolving slowly around the sun
solar wind mixes with my whisker-hairs

Caesar gets up and takes his bow and the great
black velvet curtains close

George Washington's head is so sleek and white with its
bandit eyewear like a racoon's
He poses for the dollar bill in a mask of what some
post-Revolutionary artist thinks the
Father of our Country should look like
which is why it's always so flat and unlively

You see my trickster clock is telling the truth after all
even if it's now fifteen minutes behind

as if the minute hand is stuck and the little
gulping sound it's making is actually
time at a standstill made to
compound and compound upon itself like a
potentized pill and when we

swallow the fact that all the planets move
like slow round heads on a pillow very sleepily and humming
gigantically to themselves
*(have they sound recorded the winds on Mars the upheavals on
gaseous Jupiter or the scintillating scratchiness of
Saturn's pebbly rings?)* we'll see time
face to face

I'm getting older by the minute
younger by the hour
stupider by the year
wiser by the millennium

Let love lick its glorious lips once more
and time surround the goldfish in their pond

Light shattering the air glittering with a scaly sheen

Time the trickster machine

12/18

I PRAISE YOU AND I PRIZE YOU

> *"They do not measure God with His true measure."*
> — Qur'an 6:92

I praise You and I prize You

Golden sunlight on the stairs
vine ropes hanging from trees
red sandstorms on Mars

What have we seen or heard that is
anything like You?

Elaborate calculations cannot find You

Face in the stars
wind along the ground

Ecstatic cyclones circle You
You cannot be encircled

we can only be aware

Slightest light in a coffee cup
slightest flight of the slightest fly

All the air embraces you
You cannot be embraced

Everything that lives faces you

You cannot be faced nor effaced

I can only praise and prize You

You cannot be adequately appraised

12/18

THE MYSTERY OF SOMEONE SLEEPING

The mystery of someone sleeping the
mystery of someone dead

On the train back from New York I watched
people sleeping

masks for faces eyes shut mouths lax jowls relaxed
heads lolling or wedged against windows

Where on earth have their animated inhabitants gone
leaving no trace of emotion or attitude other than

an almost embryonic fluidity of
eyelid ear cheek mouth forehead?

As if we are souls with a liquid covering that
solidifies at birth upon air contact finally

returning to fluid again when brought down
brought down to earth at last

But sleepers their faces tell no story unless
scarred

They are in a bliss they maybe don't
feel when awake they're in

God's hands as if
cradled there

ebbing and flowing
puppeted by their sleepy breathing

And I wondered at what the
sleeping face of Cleopatra must've looked like

or sleeping Jesus
all extroverted moonlight

Beauty in its essence molding
a perfect face from inside

Even these faces actually beautiful and as if
carved from within

Perfect line of lips not speaking not chattering
perfect closure of eyelids not flashing not emoting

perfect tilt of head in repose in the
soft beneficent arms of cosmos

only a spark away from the look of death
death the same face but unable to shake

awake
the spark of life between it and

final sleep looking similar to
these mortals except that unlike the dead at their

appointed station they

wake up and file out with their live faces into the

awakened world

                                                        12/19

THERE ARE A THOUSAND PASTURES

There are a thousand pastures rolling across the moon
in an inhospitable atmosphere
pockmarked like an acne'd teenager with giant
craters giants could lay their heads down in to
rest if they needed to after exhausting
space flight from some over-the-fence
galaxy a few light years away

The moon looks powdery and soft styrofoamy and
fragile up there in the black night

Decapitated head of something that's lost its head among the stars

this rolling white head that glows with
excessive saintliness after an execution
severed clean now rotating round the
earth like an eager acolyte beaming
goodness for all it's worth but charging
ocean tides with jolts of electrical push and pull
plus emotional breakers and deep
magnetic cross-currents that craze us with
love's sweet absurdities hoarse
whispers and lunar howls only

wolves on icy mountaintops truly understand
their elegant profiles in silhouette against the
intense imploring yet serene searchlight beam

of the moon

What if roaring engines raised some lunar hatches?

*What if wheels the size of Ferris Wheels were to
wobble down a lunar lane kicking up
moon dust?*

I stood here pondering this

white powder on my shoes

looking at the earth setting
the lovely cloudy earth setting

below the moon's horizon

12/23

I LEAN OUT OVER THE BALCONY OF MY BED

I lean out over the balcony of my bed
hoping to find swans gliding on a pond below
only to find rumpled covers and a coverlet
warped doorways and a
distant wall like glass through which at last

you can see where you're going and who'll be there
with you when waterfalls start pouring
rainbows across their rocks and the
sky has pointed pyramid tips descending to touch
pyramid tips in deserts provided just for that

contact whose transmission of energy
remains a mystery to all but
gliding birds and gliding whales and certain
human beings gliding unselfconsciously through
crowds on crowded city streets untouched and
untouchable

I hang out over my bed's edge
which is the embedded one inside us all
looking out onto the same territory from an
identical center

How do we love one another
if in fact we aren't resonant skin and organ obstructions
between two spaces that are really one
of pure soul

I don't know if this is clear
what I mean is
faces looking out from a central spiral
bird migrations coiling through space to a
single point

I see it's getting even more abstract

You are all inside me when I look outside
myself to you looking back
and I am inside you as well looking out

All of us are

I lean out over the edge of my bed and
trail my hand in invisible waters
rilling bubbles trill past this boat-like form that
cuts through darkness

song at high-pitched notes as if from a
tropical oratorio spontaneously sung
comes into the picture here

identity
ratatouille!

12/24

SQUIRREL-SCRATCH

Yesterday a squirrel scratched me
I was feeding stale bread to ducks and
gulls at the Haverford pond and a
fat brown squirrel scampered along the
rustic fence I held out a
slab of dry rye he swiped out of my
hands with a squirrelly swipe tall tail twitching
and in so doing inadvertently I'm absolutely
sure sliced alongside the tip of my middle finger and
along the top of the first joint of my index knuckle with his
long curved blackish
nails drawing immediate beads of
bright red blood rather copiously but didn't
stay to inspect or apologize not that I

expected him or her to but instead took
bread in claws I really saw are
little articulate long-fingered claws actually those
very same claws which admirably enable them to
run along telephone wires over busy intersections with no
teetering or uncertainty
or spiral up a
tree round and round it like a
coil in reverse shooting upward then
out on a branch leaping
across pure space to another
branch often spindly thin
with those curved black nails on those tiny
claws able to clutch at it with acrobatic

ease and so
bring him or her to safety

I love squirrels and feel no enmity to this one though it
took a while to stanch the bleeding
and the slice is still healing and slightly sore

I wonder through those beady eyes of
his or hers what he or she is

if anything
thinking

12/25

PREDICTIONS

The day was pleased that rain was predicted
as rain balls plummeted to earth

The cold front was especially gratified ceding its
central position to the warm front in its
endless do-si-do

The stock market was happy that the predicted
crash failed to happen
but the volume of shares was sliding around as predicted
stock brokers quieting their jitters with
tranquilizers with predictable side effects
glasses slipping through their hands and crashing to
parquet floors glass slivers invisibly
describing star-patterns in the
air until they landed in chaotic
told-you-so splatters invisible
in the parquet pattern underfoot

The high-profile newlywed Hollywood couple
was relieved at the tabloid prediction foretelling their
honeymoon in the Bahamas since it took place in Rome

The wheat farmers were sorry the prediction of
crop failure turned out to be true since it meant selling their
tractors and thousand acre farms to
Happy Farms Housing Developments Incorporated

The fracas of end-of-the-world predictions made

everyone secretly relieved but a little disappointed since it meant
somehow adjusting to doing the same thing every day for
another unknown stretch of time until at least
the next doomsday prediction

Angels falling in the snows of Newfoundland were
predicted and television crews were ready with
infrared lenses but only a
few dazzling snowflakes fell around a
solitary tree

Bridges to the next world were predicted to
emerge out of heaven at key points on
earth to allow everyone
safe passage over
but though some theologians and
a few splinter spiritualists were on hand with their
precise maps and timetables crinkling expectantly in their
hands only a few birds emerged swooping
so easily it seems between the two worlds
disappearing again into the
blue

I can't even predict the end of this poem exactly
though I feel the end is near

Only God can predict anything with any
accuracy but it's His
prerogative to do so then tell only His
closest friends about it who seem to

prefer blissful nonchalance in order not to
overly alarm us as we

go about our ways expecting both the
worst and the best and usually

getting something blessedly unpredictable
in between

                                                          12/26

AROUND THE FEET OF THE LORD

Even though I'm weighted down this
day this month and by emotional extension this
century everyone's elbowing their way in to immortalize
even as its wheels grind relentlessly across into the
next

About a million invisible sparks of angelic thought
rise all around us like great skirts or funnels or
even galactic worm holes that'll
slip us into a different time zone altogether

Around the feet of the Lord

On green fields as far as the eye can fathom
farther than the eye can
see
on blue fields upside-down to the sky
in which the eye sees atomic details as
clearly as ice as clearly as pain more
clearly than flame

Around the feet of the Lord

Celebration of what never existed until the
sun's warmth coaxed it from its dark den
celebration of silence in the vast cone of silence

little universes strung on gossamer threads of pure light like

abacus beads clicking in the
dark silence in the deep silence

Around the feet of the Lord

12/28

METICULOUS IN THEIR APPREHENSION MOVING

Meticulous in their apprehension moving
   forward blindly through narrow gauges
sea-wash at either side lapping as if against
      bulwarks
noses forward as if with lights on their tips
macaws flapping out of trees overhead
air filled with gnat-buzzings

The slow painful step-by-step process
saints alighting slowly in Technicolor clouds
dispensing sweet blessings with largesse

inching forward rib by rib over ridge by ridge of
rocky earth each ridge as if
etched by time's heavy labors
deeper and deeper with each
deep exhalation although crisp radiance

frames with glittering circles and
breeze-driven oblongs each elemental thing

that rocks back and forth as the crawl progresses

Here's a landscape both unearthly and real
into which our apprehenders approach with both
bravado and caution
glints in their eyes songs on their tongues moist
hearts beating Divine Names repeatedly as
water drips make soft tom-tom taps on

nerve-ends come awake with jubilant

perambulations across worlds sharper than glass

They take each thing in with motherly concern
microscopic sensitivities as if looking

down on a busy metropolis blooming alive in a
radiant gaze

12/31

PART 2

MULTIPLE LANGUAGES MULTIPLE RITUAL GESTURES

Multiple languages multiple ritual gestures in
complex dance steps the whole body moving from
side to side round and round as the
earth turns

Alaskan natives in fluffy fur parkas with taut round
frame drums they twirl in the air before
hitting with sticks
dancing figures seen from three-quarters above
against blinding snow-whiteness

Mechanics of star rotation mathematics of sidereal
moon gyration
bodies able to stand first on two legs then
rotate slowly or quickly from foot to foot

Earth light earth radiance earth alive with mortal soul torches
turning their bodies defying gravity
standing on two legs then rotating slowly or
quickly from foot to foot as the
earth turns as stars in distant
red shift pulsations turn

as night unashamedly uncloaks itself by the
moonlit heavens opening and pure

nakedness steps out onto
lengthy plains of star-bright air
extending everywhere

1/2/2000

KALEIDOSCOPE

Muscular black South Africans in silhouette against real bronze
sunrise backdrop turning white

Caribbean martial arts acrobats doing multiple back flips and
wild-leggéd windmill twists

Red Square in Moscow thronged by thousands of cheering Russians
in front of rust-red Kremlin onion domes swirling like tops
snowflakes flying upward

Huge face of coconut-shell-colored Hawaiian boy with radiating
yellow grass headdress smiling equally radiant teeth black
eyes like soft black moons in a flashing sky

Fiji Islander coming out of the sea of night with red torch held
high to light a brazier fashioned out of equally red wood shavings

Chinese president formal and tight-smiled in stiff black raincoat
pressing a button on a little metal box igniting Taoist calligraphic
fireworks of mysterious import

Hundreds of lighter-than-air lantern balloons pale yellow in the
black night let go slowly rising at angles afloat in midnight
Taiwanese sky

Drummers in black shirts and fringed white leggings stepping
gracefully over their drums while cracking drumhead wooden
sides with sticks in head-tossing happy
synchronized rhythms

Hundred-deep choruses of white-shirted Sri Lankan youths holding
lurid red lotus flowers
dark outlined almond-eyed faces solemnly smileless though singing

Strauss waltzes in Vienna great white skirts spiraling lithe
white bodies
in ballet one-two-three formations

Before Argentina waterfall cascading children's voices in Spanish
and Quechua singing *los niños de dos mil*
under a brilliant turquoise sky

Plainsong Estonian ghost-figures shrouded in the snow with long
white masks and wide-jagged-wing'd birdmen carrying
tall white crosses under blinding silvery showers of sparks

London Tower illuminated gory red by the flames of a giant
beacon ignited by a seemingly stunned Queen Elizabeth II in her
plain housewife's red overcoat and so-so pillbox hat as if
out on a supermarket shopping trip
for a box of Tetley tea-bags

Acropolis Greek chorus and orchestra men and women in florid
blue robes
among pillars of the ruined temple to Athena
on its illuminated mountaintop bathed in cobalt blue light

Palestinians with cyclone lamps tiny orange flames inside
convex glass domes in Bethlehem singing *Halleluiah* over and over
green fireworks and 2,000 white doves released simultaneously
into the sky

Chrysanthemums of light bursting to *Thus Sprach Zarathustra*
bombast and thrill

Pyramids at Giza Egyptian civilization's Seventh Millennium
long lines of men in blue gabardine business suits each with
jackal-head Anubis masks
black silhouettes of pointed snouts and pointy ears
carrying torches and striding with god-like ominous mystery
and determination

Nelson Mandela solitarily lighting a candle from his 27 years prison
cell on Robben Island
carrying it down a corridor of nakedly leaping ecstatic dancers
to hand it to the newly elected black President of South Africa

Helsinki Finland chiming midnight with 2,000 flickering candles
of hope

Shinto wedding at dawn on Japanese beach with hundreds of
drummers banging drums
bride in white kimono groom in black robes reciting marriage vows
in unison scanning down Japanese vertical calligraphy
as the rosy first-day-of-millennium
sunrise rises

Swiss fire sculpture burning hot red licks in the still-night chill black
sky of Switzerland
flame wheels slowly turning
flames flickering from circular rims

Balletic ice-skating folk dance Denmark's Tivoli Gardens lake frozen

over ladies in pink tutus lads in black breeches white socks
dancing pendulously back and forth hip and hop jolly fussy and folksy

Eiffel Tower illuminated rocket in takeoff position on earth's brave
curvature glittering disks at the different levels spinning around
then wheels of fireworks rotating up from the bottom
then spray wings flying out from the tower's sides in leaping rainbow
arcs as if breast-stroking through the sky spectacularly outwards

Brandenberg Gate searchlights back and forth black leather German
metallica rock music

Midnight bell-ringing Spain's *Puerto del Sol* fireworks display on the
red-glowing roof of the solid Greek architecture portals of government

Saint Peter's Square pop singers with microphones tuxedos and
formals His Holiness the Pope at his Plexiglas lectern
shakily delivering his millennial homily waving his hand and
looking out strangely at the assembled masses

Amplified violinist on a roof in Prague playing *Fiddler on the Roof*
with seemingly no trace of irony

Polonaise in Poland by famous Chopinesque pianist
great black grand piano covered in insulating puffy white balls of
sheep's wool like
mushrooms sprouting

Easter Island dancers in skimpy loincloths muscular limbs in the
long shadows of those giant buttress-nosed sculpture heads tilted
sightlessly heavenward

Amazon Indians on the tangly banks of the Amazon
short brown bare-breasted ladies and black-haired shamans splashily
body-painted doing a circle dance round and round each other
praying to God and asking humankind to

please preserve the rainforest

live in peace

Blue jewel in space

singing its heart out

1/2/2000

(written while watching a video of turn of the century celebrations)

LATE AND LOVELY

Late and lovely
water sounds in the pipes

sweaty in my pajamas in the Year 2000 technologically
challenged

It is late and life is lovely to me after
sleep like a tunnel grafted to my head in which I

saw pictures went on adventures
came back into this lovely world

the dreams dispersed
or *where am I going* in which

dream world?
our life so utterly short

But it has wings like corridors on either side
as wide as the world itself and wider

in which we touch Paradise
(little leaves leave imprints on our palms

and eyelids)
in these wings we dine with saints and walk on

heaven unafraid unlimited
they flap and we rise

they are eternal and then
so are we

I don't know how I know this but I can
vouch for it by butterfly by gnat by starlight

and walking these corridors is like treading
illumined water

Ah the sunlight there
fractalled rainbows drawn through straws

we sip from

I see horses as always in the
cloudy distance galloping

pinwheels

1/10

ON THE HIGH SEAS

On the high seas over a little rough water
in a dense forest in the glow of a firefly suspended
behind ancient inlaid boxes in unopened
tombs under tons of desert sand
under thickest briars and underbrush way
under even that far more under
and way back behind things far from the spotlight
behind screens and labyrinths of doors and even
disorienting tactics of blind corridors and
passageways to nowhere zig-zagging and sashaying
offshoots that almost make you think you're
getting there

But inside a complex spiderwebbing of nets within
nets inside constructs of indivisible obstacles set
one inside the other and many
others inside that
to a place now that cannot be defined almost but is
excruciatingly remote and hard-of-access
or you could say *"inside the heart of"* as in
"deep in the heart of"
or *"in the mind of"* but imbedded so
deep *"in the mind of"* as to be almost as
unreachable as a peak at the iciest tip of the
Himalayas

Or in a
microscope virus where a zillion could fit into
the dot I just dotted the "i" of "fit" with as I

wrote it out
even more remote than that

Invisible to the sight intangible to the touch
inaudible to the hearing and not at all
salty or sweet to the tongue nor
pungently tangy to the sense of smell that famous
reptilian portion of the brain like a green creature
lurking in time past brought forth into
time present by just the right combination of
odors armpit stink or civet apricot jam
bubbling in big vats on a stove and filling a
familial house with a smell that
never goes away in the nostalgic mind happy to
revive it over and over for that beady-eyed
reptile maybe more
precise than all the other senses combined

Or in the pink curl of a conch shell on an
abandoned beach in the Caribbean
or in a wisp of smoke hanging high over a
valley in the Alps a little snow-covered
hamlet way down below in a dark crevasse

Or in the eye-twinkle of a migrating butterfly as it
wings its way southward over
exhausting mileage to Brazil
or in the echo of a call one lone forest bird to
whatever other of its rare species might fly
by somewhere and be suitable
or what frog in what cold pond in cold

moonlight happy and sexual harrumphing like a
bulldog with a voice that could crack china

Elemental featheriness
desperate disappearingness
vanishment

There where there is practically nothing
maybe only a breath or two

Only a breath or two left in the whole
world of it about to
expire and the rest of the world
continuing on without it

Just a word on its lips not
"save me" or even *"goodbye"* but rather

"I am not only God is"—*"only Light is"*—

"only darkness is"— *"only this is"*— *"only this is"*—

"nothing else is"— *"only this is"*

1/11

DOWN AT THE CORNER GROCER

Down at the corner grocer
tornado in a can holocaust packaged ready to bake
cataclysm soup
you walk in
everyone's baby is there waiting to be kissed to
graduate from college to mortgage their
first house settle down die
the soda bottles are ready to pop
the proprietors are far from home
how do they like America
they barely speak the language yet do a brisk
business
milk deliveries snack chip deliveries the
ice machine the
hoodlums in their puffy parkas
you'd expect to see a mule team in the
produce aisle
a pack of wild dogs by the
packaged meats
the TV's blaring incomprehensible daytime shows
the cereal boxes are rebelling
they're forming a circle on the greasy floor
they're demanding immediate release
the breakfast cereals are so full of energy
truly dynamic ready to take on the world
the world continues its slow pace
down at the corner grocer
bicycles outside on the sidewalk
bicycles lying on their sides on the sidewalk

DOWN THE LONG ROAD

Down the long road
little preaching birds will sing of all the
good things to come
but no one will believe them

Rays out of copper-clouded skies will slant like
giant halos reversed sending all that
glory to earth to scorch all sin out
lovely fiery glory you can
wear in your hair like a halo

Down the long road
many people with epiphanies of
various intensities will throng to the Day of Joy
each of us with an epiphany suited to our
innermost natures some like crazy airplanes some
caroming on skis between pines
some through a roof of multicolored parasol rotations
some pure song and some as dark as night

Each epiphany perfect in itself like a bright
gemstone with a fountain pouring forth from
deep within it spraying messages both from
the Beyond and the Below

A source so many fathoms away the sheer
impact of receiving their messages turns us into angels
making circles where circles are needed
cubes in space with sky for sides and

oceans for windows
out of which we can see everyone looking
wistfully back at us

Down the long road
that ends where it begins and begins where it ends
that is shorter and longer than length itself with its
metric durations
and takes longer and shorter to traverse than
anything we can think of even before we've
thought it

and whose arrival is expected with an
angelic enthusiasm

the heavens already decorated for celebration

1/14

WAY DOWN IN MISSISSIPPI

Way down in Mississippi
where magnolias bloom the size of cabbages

way down along the great wall of China
where no trees have grown for a couple of millenniums

way down under
where aborigines kneel at secret waterholes

drinking the water with their silvery mouths
birds fly crickets sing their

two-part twelve-part million-part harmonies

where white handkerchiefs fly past the sun like clouds
where rain falls in spangles of nickels and dimes

where rivers overflow
like tears at the lower rims of sad lovers' eyelids

where a lone cow stands and chews
as a rainforest burns to a crisp

where nothing goes without God's knowledge
partridge pear tree snuff movie freeway

where every circle is a complete circle

a seed the size of nothing in creation

small enough to tuck under a single lover's eyelid

big enough to encompass a solar system a supernova
as an egg encompasses its yolk

as a glass encompasses its water
as an eye what it beholds

this is not mythology
our hearts like ripe golden pears hanging among

similar pendulous universes

humming like well-oiled machines spewed through space
singing like angel choirs

the seed itself up on the tip of our forefinger
not quite circular

but part and parcel of the circle after all

where magnolias bloom the size of cabbages

where trees suddenly sprout along the great wall of China

aborigines kneel and make soft lapping sounds with their lips

birds fly crickets sing multifarious rhythmings

handkerchiefs fly rain falls rivers rise lovers cry

a cow stands methodically chewing

every circle is a complete circle

God knows

every circle is a circular circle

God knows

                                                          1/15

I GOT SHOT TO DEATH

I got shot to death
so I plucked the bullet out of my flesh
and swallowed it
it became a rose
incandescent bloom in the belly of the world
purple and red swirls of rose petals filling the sky
fields of beauty so rare where no one dares walk
crystalline mountainsides and domes of glass
domes of fluttering doves against domes of cut glass
against high domes of diamond that vanish into sheer exuberance

I got shot to death
and as I fell I fell forward off the world
into canyons of lies down and down past
walls of steep verticality slick as ice
deeper to our origins through phyla and fauna
where wailing takes place and loud groans and
dark soul's lamentation below rivers of black
tar and rivers of slick black silk
farther and farther as I fell I found I was
flying forward and come to you now
shot to death and singing

The bullet pierced me in a vital place
putting a direct stop to whatever it was I was
going to do

It's such a door slam
it's such a permanent change of pace

I was going up hill now I'm going down
or out along not an incline as much as a
spreading where there was tightness
light where there was cramped space with too little air

Dead now I feel I'm ready for anything
kiss me with that rose of your own death my
dearest one that rose field of black and purple
blooms
rose aromas lift you

I was shot to death and that was it
the kaleidoscope of worlds collapsed back into me with
all its rainbow colors flashing
spiraling to a tight center
sucking in distant starlight along the way
to a tight center that as I rose became
a seeing eye a wolf's eye in the arctic
a single eye afloat along a blinding white tundra where
silence is the only sound there is
and sight the only seeing

I got shot to death and swallowed God my dear ones
O all my dear ones

I swallowed God my dear ones
O all my dear ones

1/16

LOVE SONG

OK the music that should accompany this
poem is a wailing wolf howl a fire engine
siren and a big gong
for love

Love that catapults off the top of a building at
top speed and back-flips past Niagara Falls
cascades with spectacular strobe-effect of the
heart's shuttering motion dark and light which of
course is tantamount to ecstasy

The music here being the fire engine siren

Love that tears the heart out of the body to use as
stationary upon which to write unreadable
nonsense with blood red ink and a pen that is all the
poor lover's physique up to this point as if all the
bedridden illnesses and slow recoveries were
just for this moment of lovesickness alone

*The music here being the howling wolf alone
howling mournfully on a mountain peak for its pack*

Love that slaps the buttocks of a whole
herd of deer in the moonlight so that they
all take off at once as one bounding
body across fields of snow up hill into
the furnace of a forest fire as if they didn't know any
better the best of them as well as the

worst of them toasting to a crisp *that's
love!* hooves first into the flames

*The music here is the resonating arcs of the airwaves of a
giant gong*

Love that stands up that stalks across the
room in the grip of an inspiration that dares to
look hollow-eyed into a mirror and see
a flame-tip burst blue then black with
rage then incandescent red with unbearable joy

A love that may be human-based and
lust-origin'd but that very quickly and
authentically is exacerbated into

a divine love as if ignited by God's own match
for God's own reasons to light up one
bomb-blasted citadel for worship out of the
whole war-torn suburb during
actual bombing

the faces of the beloveds torches enough
to light the way to the door of it
and through it into the smoking silent room facing
a wall-less vista overlooking valleys and
waterfalls incandescently blue and green and silver-sky'd

*The music here being all three
the wolf's loneliest wail the siren's most
soul-gripping scream and a final*

gong-sound dying away over every other

as love's music fades into audible silence
a wisp at a time a sound so much a pure

echo of itself after all

you wonder if it ever existed in itself after all

or only

as an echoing memory

                                                    1/18

WE'RE A TRIBE OF FISH HEAD NAVIGATORS

We're a tribe of fish head navigators
we're the bone people lost on the moon
we've got knives in our boots in the shapes of small tuning forks
we've got multicolored faces that turn toward the sun
at all the right times

We've all fallen in love and out of it again in a wink
and our nervous systems like spider webs
stretch across space to catch whomever
unsuspecting zeros in

If it's a matter of commerce no one wins
we all ride a birch-bark canoe into green mist at last
when the moose with an angel face
appears and tips its horns

Hardly before we've finally arrived we suddenly have to go
leaving a forest of red and black flags at half mast and a
floor of excessively wrinkled papers and smudged
documents and an open window onto the
waterfall

down which everything that's ever existed or exists or will exist
in slow-motion fuzzy focus
including ourselves
washes over

1/20

LIPS CAN'T

Lips can't really well pronounce it
fig leaf orange rind simple stone

Hands can barely write it out
black of night light of day

Bodies make a brave contortion
Samothrace wingéd David naked

Eyes can almost indicate it
beacons flashing at the end of land

Hearts in their interior song
I see a meadow opening slowly

Blood that pours like a stunned Niagara
pumping in a double pulse

Deep in the heart of the heart alone
where everyone is solitary

Facing the central cornerstone
recognized and acknowledged

Name pronounceable still mysterious
mirror soaring through outer space

Cosmic curve that seems to smile
giant hole like an opening eye

O lente lente currite noctis equi
Slowly slowly run you horses of the night

waves of it splashing at our feet

How can we not walk through its light
on our tongues before we speak

In our hands before we write
in our bodies as they bend

In our eyes in dark and light
in our hearts unveiled light

                                              1/24

THE CLOTH THAT REFUSED TO BE WASHED

Once upon a time someone wove a piece of cloth
but when they had it made into a shirt and
wore it then wanted to wash it
it refused to be washed
it struggled and curled and flapped and finally
flew away like newspaper in the wind
and came down on a rock resolutely refusing to let
water touch it

The man who had made the shirt didn't
know what to do
he looked with confusion at the cloth then tried
various methods to get it washed
even sneaking up on it from behind with a
bucket of hot sudsy water
splashing it on the cloth as it lay on the rock
but before the water could hit it that
stubborn sly and canny cloth curled away and the
water washed the rock instead the cloth
crumpled in more dirt at its base

In fact it got dirtier and dirtier and absolutely
no amount of stealth could overtake its
refusal to get washed
the man was shirtless
he had to wear the shirt dirty or not
he shook it brushed it snapped it in the air to
shake off the dirt but naturally the
cloth which was white to begin with began to

lose its whiteness to a whole rainbow history of
spills and mishaps and the natural
rubbing against the soiled walls of life
until the shirt really was a flag of
the past almost like a map of its owner's
actions and reactions foibles weaknesses and darkness
cat-hair a grease spot a coffee stain one little
patch of the original whiteness but no longer a
brilliant white which it could get if it only would
submit to some hot water and soap
that pristine original state of the present
which would redeem it from its past and give it a
future perhaps I'm getting a little too
theological here but at any rate

One day the shirt was hanging on a hook and getting
progressively left behind by the man who made another
shirt out of an old sheet which allowed the weekly
washing without protest

and a rosy shirt went by in the dark corner where the old shirt
hung a bright flowered red and green and purple
splashy print affair that excited the cloth of the
once-white shirt until it wriggled and wrenched and finally
flipped off its hook and with a kind of
textile longing in its warp and woof
dragged itself across the
dirt floor of the poor man's hut
(I'm thinking Mexico as I write this)

and managed to knock down a glass of water that had been

left on the floor by one of the man's
children and lay there as the water
splashed on an edge enough to
wet it completely and even wash away at least a
tiny fraction of its dirt
for love of the flowery shirt
for love of its roses red and green and purple

It never saw that shirt again but it
waited for it every time the man wore it
gleaming white again at the market or in the
village square the white shirt keeping its
eye out for the other one to pass by
the eye of its buttonhole perhaps
I don't know
the eye of its simple consciousness of itself as a
shirt and not a
sewing machine

the shirt that refused to get washed until its
reason for refusal evaporated
for a greater love than itself

until it grew old and threadbare and got
patched and re-sewn and new
buttons put on and then made into
patches itself on a full ruffly skirt for his wife and found itself
next to a patch that had
red and green and purple roses on it

It was finally united with its beloved!

and the wind blew through them and

rippled and rustled them both as his
wife worked or danced or walked to the marketplace

or threw it in a heap for washing
or as she appeared to her husband naked as light

as clean as the day she was born

as clean as a cloth that's submitted to washing

in the darkened room

                                                            1/24

FIRST MILLENNIAL BLIZZARD

The first deep blizzard of the new millennium
makes everything furry and rounded
like the wide velvet mat of a jeweler
but instead of black it's ermine fluffily covering everything
you'd expect to see giant diamonds or a few
cut emeralds float down from the silvery sky
joining the extravagant glitter with glitter upon glitter

The streets are desolate
in the deep interiors of their houses everyone's turned to stone
or interior dialogs
or saints on their knees in their icy cells at prayer
or sexual acrobats in gaudy Technicolor rooms with fur
or under colorful afghans and blankets reading thick dog-eared second hand
novels by second rate novelists

Herds of mythic giant white horses could
rage through the streets kicking up snow
giant futuristic metal cars with huge searchlights
mounted on their Darth Vader hoods could
ominously patrol the snow roads
driven by thick-bicep'd Viking types laughing uproariously at the silence

which falls down over everything and
swallows it up like a

wet lozenge on the bright red tongue of a

sick person silently and slowly

dying to this world in order to rise

triumphantly into the next

                                                                          1/26

AND OF ALL THE TEN THOUSAND THINGS

And of all the ten thousand things to be
grateful for
there's water in the tap ink in this pen blood in these
veins love in your eyes
air molecules float freely
nourishing our air-hungry cells to provide
aerated heavenly qualities as of
flight and buoyancy

But gravity's also to be grateful for
that things fall earthward
though our souls quite often
and when we die float airily upward or outward
becoming more radically inward than ever
though at that point the distinction may seem to evaporate

Grateful for light as always that may or may not
be affected by gravity
it also bathes us inwardly and outwardly
is the definite deodorant of the soul
we pass through it and it passes through us
simultaneously
onto fields of praise

Then there's moonlight to contend with and sunlight
how they mingle and join and arrive at our
tables with attendant starlight in
crunchily edible digestible forms
starlight running through our bodies like swift schools of

lightning-flash fish through Caribbean channels
across deep pink coral reefs

What's to be grateful for?

Gratitude itself

to the Giver's endless generous largesse

I'm sitting in my bed happily enumerating and my
mind's like an ocean throwing silvery surf against

huge rocks solid as night that

even like night itself gradually disperse into

mist

in a watery

dawn

2/2

ABOUT THE AUTHOR

Born in 1940 in Oakland, California, Daniel Abdal-Hayy Moore's first book of poems, *Dawn Visions*, was published by Lawrence Ferlinghetti of City Lights Books, San Francisco, in 1964, and the second in 1972, *Burnt Heart/Ode to the War Dead*. He created and directed *The Floating Lotus Magic Opera Company* in Berkeley, California in the late 60s, and presented two major productions, *The Walls Are Running Blood*, and *Bliss Apocalypse*. He became a Sufi Muslim in 1970, performed the Hajj in 1972, and lived and traveled throughout Morocco, Spain, Algeria and Nigeria, landing in California and publishing *The Desert is the Only Way Out*, and *Chronicles of Akhira* in the early 80s (Zilzal Press). Residing in Philadelphia since 1990, in 1996 he published *The Ramadan Sonnets* (Jusoor/City Lights), and in 2002, *The Blind Beekeeper* (Jusoor/Syracuse University Press). He has been the major editor for a number of works, including *The Burdah* of Shaykh Busiri, translated by Shaykh Hamza Yusuf, and the poetry of Palestinian poet, Mahmoud Darwish, translated by Munir Akash. He is also widely published on the worldwide web: *The American Muslim, DeenPort*, and his own website and poetry blog, among others: www.danielmoorepoetry.com, www.ecstaticxchange.wordpress.com. He is also currently poetry editor for *Seasons Journal* and *Islamica Magazine*. The Ecstatic Exchange Series is bringing out the extensive body of his poetry (a complete list of published works on page 2).

POETIC WORKS by Daniel Abdal-Hayy Moore
Published and Unpublished
(many to appear in The Ecstatic Exchange Series)

Dawn Visions (published by City Lights, 1964)
Burnt Heart/Ode to the War Dead (published by City Lights, 1972)
This Body of Black Light Gone Through the Diamond (printed by Fred Stone, Cambridge, Mass, 1965)
On The Streets at Night Alone (1965?)
All Hail the Surgical Lamp (1967)
States of Amazement (1970)

Abdallah Jones and the Disappearing-Dust Caper (published by The Ecstatic Exchange/Crescent Series, 2006)
'Ala ud-Deen and the Magic Lamp
The Chronicles of Akhira (1981) (published by Zilzal Press with Typo glyphs by Karl Kempton, 1986)
Mouloud (1984) (A Zilzal Press chapbook, 1995)
Man is the Crown of Creation (1984)
The Look of the Lion (The Parabolas of Sight) (1984)
The Desert is the Only Way Out (completed 4/21/84) (Zilzal Press chapbook, 1985)
Atomic Dance (1984) (am here books, 1988)
Outlandish Tales (1984)
Awake as Never Before (12/26/84) (Zilzal Press chapbook, 1993)
Glorious Intervals (1/1/85) (Zilzal Press chapbook, ?)
Long Days on Earth/Book I (1/28 – 8/30/85)
Long Days on Earth/Book II (Hayy Ibn Yaqzan)
Long Days on Earth/Book III (1/22/86)
Long Days on Earth/Book IV (1986)
The Ramadan Sonnets (Long Days on Earth/Book V) (5/9 – 6/11/86) (Published by Jusoor/City Lights Books, 1996) (Republished as Ramadan Sonnets by The Ecstatic Exchange, 2005)
Long Days on Earth/Book VI (6-8/30/86)
Holograms (9/4/86 – 3/26/87)
History of the World (The Epic of Man's Survival) (4/7 – 6/18/87)
Exploratory Odes (6/25 – 10/18/87)
The Man at the End of the World (11/11 – 12/10/87)

The Perfect Orchestra (3/30 – 7/25/88)
Fed from Underground Springs (7/30 – 11/23/88)
Ideas of the Heart (11/27/88 – 5/5/89)
New Poems (scattered poems, out of series, from 3/24 – 8/9/89)
Facing Mecca (5/16 – 11/11/89)
A Maddening Disregard for the Passage of Time (11/17/89 – 5/20/90)
The Heart Falls in Love with Visions of Perfection (6/15/90 – 6/2/91)
Like When You Wave at a Train and the Train Hoots Back at You (Farid's Book) (6/11 – 7/26/91) (Published by The Ecstatic Exchange, 2008)
Orpheus Meets Morpheus (8/1/91– 3/14/92)
The Puzzle (3/21/92 – 8/17/93)
The Greater Vehicle (10/17/93 – 4/30/94)
A Hundred Little 3-D Pictures (5/14/94 – 9/11/95)
The Angel Broadcast (9/29 – 12/17/95)
Mecca/Medina Time-Warp (12/19/95 – 1/6/96) (Published as a Zilzal Press chapbook, 1996)
Miracle Songs for the Millennium (1/20 – 10/16/96)
The Blind Beekeeper (11/15/96 – 5/30/97) (Published 2002 by Jusoor/Syracuse University Press)
Chants for the Beauty Feast (6/3 – 10/28/97)
You Open a Door and it's a Starry Night (10/29/97 – 5/23/98)
Salt Prayers (5/29 – 10/24/98) (Published by The Ecstatic Exchange, 2005)
Some (10/25/98 – 4/25/99)
Flight to Egypt (5/1 – 5/16/99)
I Imagine a Lion (5/21 – 11/15/99) (Published by The Ecstatic Exchange, 2006)
Millennial Prognostications (11/25/99 – 2/2/2000) (Published by The Ecstatic Exchange, 2009)
The Book of Infinite Beauty (2/4 – 10/8/2000)
Blood Songs (10/9/2000 – 4/3/2001)
The Music Space (4/10 – 9/16/2001) (Published by The Ecstatic Exchange, 2007)
Where Death Goes (9/20/2001 – 5/1/2002)
The Flame of Transformation Turns to Light (99 Ghazals Written in English) (5/14 – 8/21/2002) (Published by The Ecstatic Exchange, 2007)
Through Rose-Colored Glasses (7/22/2002 – 1/15/2003) (Published by

The Ecstatic Exchange, 2007)
Psalms for the Broken-Hearted (1/22 – 5/25/2003) (Published by The Ecstatic Exchange, 2006)
Hoopoe's Argument (5/27 – 9/18/03)
Love is a Letter Burning in a High Wind (9/21 – 11/6/2003) (Published by The Ecstatic Exchange, 2006)
Laughing Buddha/Weeping Sufi (11/7/2003 – 1/10/2004) (Published by The Ecstatic Exchange, 2005)
Mars and Beyond (1/20 – 3/29/2004) (Published by The Ecstatic Exchange, 2005)
Underwater Galaxies (4/5 – 7/21/2004) (Published by The Ecstatic Exchange, 2007)
Cooked Oranges (7/23/2004 – 1/24/2005 (Published by The Ecstatic Exchange, 2007)
Holiday from the Perfect Crime (1/25 – 6/11/2005)
Stories Too Fiery to Sing Too Watery to Whisper (6/13 – 10/24/2005)
Coattails of the Saint (10/26/2005 – 5/10/2006) (Published by The Ecstatic Exchange, 2006)
In the Realm of Neither (5/14/2006 – 11/12/06) (Published by The Ecstatic Exchange, 2008)
Invention of the Wheel (11/13/06 – 6/10/07)
The Sound of Geese Over the House (6/15 – 11/4/07)
The Fire Eater's Lunchbreak (11/11/07 – 5/19/2008) (Published by The Ecstatic Exchange, 2008)
Sparks Off the Main Strike (5/24/2008 – 1/10/2009)

www.ingramcontent.com/pod-product-compliance
Lightning Source LLC
Chambersburg PA
CBHW032207040426
42449CB00005B/484